A Life

Contemplated in Senryu, Poems & Haiku

Dr David H. Dighton

MEDICAUSE

First Published 2025

Copyright © David Henry Dighton

David H. Dighton™

All rights reserved. No part of this publication may be reproduced or transmitted in any form or by any means, electronic or mechanical, including photocopy, recording or any information storage and retrieval systems, without the permission in writing from the publisher, author or under licence from the Copyright Licensing Agency Ltd.

The text is not to be used without permission for training AI programs. models or applications of any sort.

Published in the UK by MediCause, 115 High Rd., Loughton, Essex. UK. IG10 4JA

www.daviddighton.com

email: david@daviddighton.com

British Library Cataloguing in Publication Data

A CIP catalogue record for this title is available from the British Library.

ISBN: 978-1-0683597-4-3

About the Author

Formerly,

British Heart Foundation Research Fellow,

St. George's Hospital, London.

Lecturer in Cardiology,

Charing Cross Hospital, London.

Chef de Clinique, Cardiologist, Vrije Universiteit. Amsterdam.

Former Director: Cardiac Centre. Loughton. Essex, UK.

www.daviddighton.com

email:

david@daviddighton.com

Dr. David H. Dighton qualified at the London Hospital Medical College in 1966 with MB and BS (London) degrees. In 1970, after a year or so in NHS general practice, he became a British Heart Foundation Fellow in Cardiology at St. George's Hospital, Hyde Park Corner, London, working with cardiologists Dr. Aubrey Leatham and Dr. Alan Harris. In 1973, he became a MRCP(UK), and later a Lecturer (London University) in Medicine and Cardiology at Charing Cross Hospital, London.

In 1980, as Chef de Clinique (Assistant Professor) at the Vrije University Hospital, Amsterdam, he helped introduce transvenous pacing and collaborated in ongoing coronary artery research. After returning to the UK in 1982, he worked both in his own private medical and cardiac practice in Loughton, Essex (The Loughton Clinic, established in 1973), undertaking invasive cardiac investigations at the Wellington Hospital, London. In 2000, he started a private cardiac diagnostic centre, specialising in the early detection and prevention of coronary artery disease (The Cardiac Centre, Loughton). This closed, once the Public Services Authority directed the GMC to withdraw his license to practice in the UK (for the political reasons are detailed in his book, *'The NHS. Our Sick Sacred Cow.' 2023).* As an independent private cardiologist and general physician, he disagreed with UK medical bureaucracy, and who they thought most qualified to devise, regulate and supervise medical practice; opinions he based on having been a medical student, general physician and cardiologist for sixty years.

In 2003 and 2006, he wrote two books on food and the heart, and between 2022 and 2025, seven books on medical and cardiac subjects. His latest books (2025), explore the possible neurophysiological and everyday bases for tiredness, fatigue and exhaustion. This is his twelfth book (see list of works by the author for details). He continues to publish books on cardiac topics, to write haiku and to research cardiac prevention.

His interest in the frontier that lies between art and science in medical practice, led to his magnum opus. *The Art and Science of Medical Practice,* details not only what he was taught by many experienced physicians, but what he learned from practising both the art and science of medicine in teaching hospitals and in private practice. As medical student, physician and cardiologist, he studied and worked within the fold of the UK medical profession for sixty years.

He has other interests. He is a poor linguist but loves learning languages and communicating in languages other than his mother tongue. He draws and paints in oils on canvas. For his own amusement, he plays the guitar and piano. He likes to compose simple melodies, one of which introduces his YouTube videos for patients on understanding heart problems (Dr. Dighton interviews). Another he played live for a friend on Facebook.

For further information go to:

www.daviddighton.com

Email: david@daviddighton.com.

Previous Works

Eat to Your Heart's Content. The diet and lifestyle for a healthy heart.(2003). HeartShield.

ISBN: 0-9551072-0-2

HeartSense. How to look after your heart.(2006). HeartShield.

ISBN: 0-9551072-1-0

The NHS: Our Sick Sacred Cow: Causes and Cures (2023)

Paperback. ISBN: 978-1-3999-6027-4 (also ebook from: https://stan.store/drdhd001001)

How to Become Heart-Smart. A User's Guide to Heart Health and Heart Disease Prevention. (2023; 1st Ed./**2nd Ed. 2024**. ISBN: 978-1-3999-7461-5 (also ebook from: https://stan.store/drdhd001001)

Who Loses Wins. Winning Weight Loss Battles: A 'Fat Mentality' v A 'Fit Mentality' (2024).

Paperback ISBN: 978-1-7385207-1-8; ebook: 978-1-7385207-2-5. (from: https://stan.store/drdhd001001)

Doctors, Nurses & Patients. How to Survive Medical Practice (2024). ISBN: Paperback: 978-1-7385207-5-6; ebook: 978-1-7385207-6-3 ((from: https://stan.store/drdhd001001)

The Art and Science of Medical Practice (2024). ISBN: (hardback: 978-1-7385207-7-0;

Paperback: 978-1-7385207-3-2; ebook: 978-1-7385207-4-9 (from: https://stan.store/drdhd001001)

Poems for Recycling Lives (2024).

ISBN: Paperback: 978-1-7385207-8-7; ebook: 978-1-7385207-9-4

Essential Adult Cardiology. A Textbook for Aspiring Cardiologists.(2025)

ISBN: Hardback 978-0683597-0-5; Paperback 978-0683597-2-9; e-book 978-0683597-1-2

Tiredness, Chronic Fatigue and Exhaustion. Neurophysiology and Cardiovascular Risk. (2025).

Hardback only. ISBN: 978-1-0683597-3-6

Tired All the Time. Causes, Consequences and Cures. (2025)

Hardback ISBN: 9781068359743; Paperback ISBN: 9781068359750; E-book ISBN: 9781068359767

Goto: www.daviddighton.com for more information

Dedication

For all those who question the essence of their being.

Contents

Detailed Contents	XV
Introduction	1
PART ONE	4
1. Contemplations	5
PART TWO	44
2. Essence of Being	45
PART THREE	68
3. Getting Personal	69
PART FOUR	112
4. Them or Us?	113

Index   135

Detailed Contents

Contemplations

Friendship (p5); Time (p6); More Time (p7); Blessed Time (p8); Beauty (p9); Discipline (p10); Public Interest (p12); Dilemma and Fatigue (p13); Can Truth Set Us Free? (p14); Discovery (p15); False Accusation (p15); In Homage to Socrates (p16); Minds at Work (p18); The Knowable (p20); What Ruins Lives? (p21); Fooling Our-self? (p22); Hunter-Gathering Still? (p23); Why Not Imperfection? (p23); New Era (p24); Going Unnoticed (p25); The Colour of Meaning (p27); Fearsome (p28); Once Balanced (p29); Open-Minded (p31); Predictability (p32); Remember Wittgenstein? (p33); Wisdom (p34); Resolution (p36);

Nothing to Lose (p37); Who Cares? (p37); If Angels Watch (p38); Species of Man (p38); Graduation (p39); Maturation (p40); Skin (p41); Clarity (p41); Vigilance (p42); Positive and Negative (p43); Yet Another Delusion? (p43).

On the Essence of Being

On the Essence of Being (p45); Light & Dark (p47); Love (p48); Spiritual Presence? (p49); Let's Call it: 'Zhe' ж (Poem) (p51); The Quest (p61); Essence (p62); Lying Between the Definable (p64); Our Essence (p64); Essence of Reality (p65); Togetherness (p67).

Getting Personal

Shattered Love (p69); Restoration (p71); Knowing Nothing (p71); Linger No Longer (p72); Reliability (p72); Entangled Love (p73); Never Relevant? (p74); Missed Opportunity? (p75); Giving & Taking (p77); Breaking Bonds (p79); Love's Return? (p80); Existence (p81); How to Live Life (p81); Defining a Friend (p82); A Doctor's Demise (p83); Readiness (p84); Imagination (p84); Try! (p85); The Blessed (p86); Time & Place (p89); Which Place? (p90); Achievement (p90); Progressing (p91); Sexual Gratification (p92); Multiplying Stress (p93); Leave Hubris Behind? (p94); Young & Old (p96); Blame Complexity? (p97); Expressed Emotion (p98); A State of Grace (p99); Alone? (p101); Breaking Ego (p102); Simplicity Reigns (p102); Does Age Define Us? (p104); Understanding (p105); Shop or Not? (p106); Forsaken Time (p106); Suffering;? (p107); One Enchanted Evening (p108); Onward (p109); A Cause of Discord (p109); Oh Carol(e), I Am But A Fool! (p110); Strength (p111);

Them & Us

Cultural Mix (p113); No Time? (p115); Detachment (p115); Nagged (p116); A Past Life (p117); Forgiveness (p117); Aspects of Sanctimony (p119); Engagement (p119); Engaging? (p121); From Pre-History (p122); Toddlers' Despair (p124); Why Charlie Kirk? (p125); Solitude; (p126) Religion (p126); Insecurity (p127); Find and Seek (p127); Dreams (p129); Inhumanity (poem) (p130).

Introduction

This is my second offering of haiku-like poems. These are also about life and living – about the essence of human existence; the essence of being – of love, understanding, human interaction and fate.

I have tried to capture the idea of an 'essence' to life; not just that which pervades the whole physical universe, but that sub-set focussed entirely on our human existence as sentient beings.

In one long poem, I challenge the romantic among us to address the physical essence of being; those insisted on by science and mathematical expression – that boxed-in, hierarchical pyramid of logic, devoid of any fictional romanticism. Both co-exist of course, but the better we understand both, the clearer will be our insight into what essence percolates our existence.

At the moment, romantics can ignore science and scientists if they want, and romantic ideas never need concern any basic scientist.

Fortunately, there has never been any need to certify the free-thinking polymath: one capable of glimpsing beyond the binary; beyond the use of pigeon holes and check-boxes; one able to embrace free-thinking beyond algorithm, embracing both science and fiction.

Both romantics and scientists are happy in their isolation, of course. I am not. The literary romantics can gain self-esteem from manufacturing fiction, translating life into engaging narratives. Scientists, on the other hand, sanctimoniously disallow anything romantic, philosophic or conjectural, in their formal thinking. In private, of course, many (apart from their many esteemed autistic bedfellows) much enjoy wandering among the romantics. Bridging the gap is important to me, and so I have tried to express both the divide and the connection between them, here in these works.

My efforts here are best called 'Senryu', not traditional 'Haiku' (given they are neither about nature, nor do they have a 3-line format). Whether alone or grouped together as senryu poems, each short piece has a 17-syllable format. I have retained this for two reasons. I regard brevity as a desirable discipline. This, together with that other essential component of correct thinking and understanding – clarity – define all haiku and senryu construction.

In any collection of thoughts like this, there will be only a few that will resonate for each person. Our search for appropriate knowledge and direction is always a similar quest. My aim is for each reader to find at least one item they regard as a gem; one that speaks to them and enables a better understanding and extra insight into life.

PART ONE

Chapter One

Contemplations

Friendship

Unwavering loyalty:
One prized gift;
But only from –
True friendship

Time

Transported by words:
Time slips away,
And our journey,
Becomes shorter.

As time slips by,
Life, transported,
Slips ever closer
To certainty.

More Time

Time passes

Relentlessly –

Persistently:

Stopped only by death.

Soon, nothing old

Will be known;

Soon to be bypassed

By sparkling newness.

Blessed Time

I have been blessed
To live through black
And white:
To colour media.

I have been blessed,
Living with conversation –
Before screens,
And reels.

I have been blessed
To live through times
Of honour, dignity,
And grace.

Are we now,
To live only with
Eroded standards;
Fame and gain?

Beauty

Beware of beauty:
Its ego and allure;
Their power –
Together.

Beauty itself,
Will sometimes

Obscure intelligence –
But not often.

Combined they are:
So rarely constructive,
So commonly –

Destructive.

Discipline

Many no longer
Esteem knowledge;
Honour, excellence,
Or respect.

Profit,
And vulgarity,
Garlanded by wealth,
Draw acclamation.

As discipline and
Education decline,
The feral
Multiply

As order
Disintegrates:
Disciplined foreigners
Will overtake.

And so,
All empires collapse,
And are rebuilt
Using strict compliance.

Hence,
The observant,
And all the faithful with power,
Will have their day.

Realising
How incorrect
Is bio-equality:
They win.

Public Interest

Subsume humanity,
In the name of
Public interest,
And good?

Dilemma and Fatigue

The stress of a
Dilemma:
Creates a state of
Preoccupation.

Early waking,
Daytime tiredness,
And failing
Coordination.

The solution resolved,
Brings calm;
Restful sleep,
And tranquillity.

Can Truth Set Us Free?

Most live their lives,
Ruled by vanity.
So truth,
Liberates their rage.

Realists,
Need the truth.
It sets them free,
From a life of fantasy.

Discovery

Exploring the world,
Wide and far,
Will often lead
Us to solitude.

Exploring –
Benefits us most,
When we discover
Our real selves.

False Accusation

False accusation:
Equals the crime,
And deserves
Retribution.

Homage to Socrates

Are not:

Grace and harmony,

The twin sisters,

Of goodness and virtue?

Art can bring,

Beauty and Grace:

To eye and ear,

Like an health-giving breeze.

Beautiful souls:

Harmonising with

Beauty of form –

The fairest sight.

Pleasure deprives man,

As much of his faculty,

As will,

Sensing pain.

Minds at Work

Lowest common denominator:

Minds,

That never have,

Left the womb.

Limited minds,

Thought OK,

Have never seen –

Outside their back garden.

. . . Free to create,

With every feeling:

Subject to

Unchecked bias.

A LIFE

Expansive minds,

Have travelled;

Learned and created

Intelligibly.

Mature minds,

Have judgement and openness,

And are at-one

With themselves.

The Knowable

Consciousness,

Is a complex function –

Of

Neuronal activity.

Knowable;

Conceivable;

Unpredictable;

Inescapable.

What Ruins Lives?

Resentment and anger;

Indignation and guilt –

Can all,

Ruin lives.

With open benevolence,

Love,

And at-oneness,

Our lives are fulfilled.

Fooling Our-Self?

Knowing if,

We are fooling ourselves;

Rests on data,

And the art of choice.

Pigeon-holing,

And sorting:

Ordered, but leaves

Reality unchanged.

Hunter-Gathering Still?

Getting rich,

Is hunter-gathering:

And as primitive

As ever.

Why Not Imperfection?

If perfection,

Has never existed:

Why avoid

Imperfection?

New Era?

New era:

True power acts,

While politicians

Can only tinker.

The dissident,

Will continue:

To raise hell,

Until gaining control.

Going Unnoticed

How many

Of the unnoticed,

Will deserve,

Some notability?

How many of those,

Who are widely known,

Would wish:

Anonymity?

The self-promoting,

Vain and egoist,

Will disregard,

These questions.

Lying dormant there,

Within un-marked youth,

Lies un-sparked

Potential.

Sparks come,

Only from the inspired:

Those whose hands -

Both carry lit torches.

The Colour of Meaning

Meaning varies with the colour,

Language paints.

Words convey:

Conception.

Fearsome

Nothing competes

With fear:

To poison our hope,

And imprison our mind.

Fear once overcome,

Can release our joy,

Engendering:

Shock and magic.

A LIFE

Once Balanced

With balance,

In all dimensions;

Deceit and hate,

Cannot perturb us.

At-oneness,

Has no fractions.

Achieving contentment,

Takes one prime step.

For most of us,

The chasm,

Is too wide:

Some unable to approach.

Not all,

Will reach the end:

Of maturation;

Of fulfilled *shu-ha-ri*.

Open-Minded

Behold:

A selfless man.

Open-minded,

Needing to know nothing more.

There are

Different universes:

Each of us exists,

In our own.

Predictability

The brick:

Its shape, but not size,

Must subtend:

Everything we build with it.

Knowing each brick,

Predicts structure;

But, only complexity,

Adds awe.

Complexity:

Embodied in us,

Is a frontier,

We must accept.

Remember Wittgenstein?

By agreement,

Words have assigned meaning.

But more,

Suffuses the gaps.

The context,

And some conjecture,

Can together help,

Understanding.

Wisdom

Without understanding,

Knowledge alone,

Never formulates

Wisdom.

Genuine stupidity,

Like genuine wisdom,

Flies

Unaided.

False wisdom,

Like false stupidity,

Can be funny,

Or dangerous.

The simplest of us

Can be wise;

And the most intelligent,

Stupid.

Resolution

Our world,

Now has three emperors;

Many kings,

Princes and many pawns.

When two emperors,

Decide fate:

All pawns and kings,

Capitulate.

Nothing to Lose

Real security –

Means nothing to lose;

Or money for

Defences!

Who Cares?

Is it true:

Nobody cares?

Or is it true:

That only the good care?

If Angels Watch

Must angels watch,

Good and evil?

Benevolence;

Inhumanity?

Species of Man

Each species of man,

Has a different focus,

Within their being.

Some in their body;

Some within emotion;

Some within cognition.

Graduation

Achievement!

Hubris and pride.

Add esteem and joy,

To shape her future.

The future -

Shapes now in pencil:

Awaiting some colour,

And some depth.

A new crossroad:

One frontier ending,

A new front beginning

In limbo.

Maturation

The young wait,

For something to happen.

The old wait,

While nothing happens.

Age may chase youth,

But youth knows not,

What youth needs most –

Some maturity.

Skin

As pale chases tan,

And black wants pallor;

Vanity supports

Discord.

Clarity

The mastery
Of all art,
And all action,
Derives from clarity.

Through the mist,
Beauty loses impact;
Through the mist,
Clarity is lost.

Vigilance

Metal will rust;
Baths overflow;
Strokes happen,
Without fixed attention.

Focus and clarity,
Will serve prevention;
Defying
Entropy.

Otherwise:
The ground will shift,
With absence of purpose,

Beneath our feet.

Positive and Negative

Positivity –
Can save a life,
And encourage,
Your self-esteem.

Suffering

Unrelenting negativity,
Can threaten your
Life.

Yet Another Delusion?

History,
Is not ours:
Sensing past suffering -
A delusion.

PART TWO

CHAPTER TWO

Essence of Being

On the Essence of Being

From ethereal space,
Poets can touch
Meaning,
To give us insight.

This essence –

Sensed always:

In music, poems,

And in loving glances.

Is detected in touch,

And in a portrait:

To mean more,

Than just words.

Light & Dark

The essence

Of morning:

Vibrant early light,

Silent in air and dew.

The essence

Of dusk,

Comes silent and fading:

Calling for night rhythms.

Love

The essence

Of new found love,

Comes held in one gaze:

Transfixed by one touch.

The essence stays;

Despite,

All else going:

Other lives to lead and share.

The essence of their soul;

Like their fragrance,

Lingers beyond

Their presence.

Spiritual Presence?

Birds tweet,

Far beyond the roar:

Yet,

Far beyond perception and thinking.

Singing birds,

Unheard across the noise:

Their lives,

And existence denied.

Might spirits –

Voices of the past,

Speak so soft,

That life and noise can drown them?

Let's Call it 'Zhe' (ж).

Not the sound of the cosmos in repose:

Inaudible –

Yet, buzzing with energy;

Existence guessed – not perceived:

Not even by collective consciousness;

Perhaps too fleeting to comprehend.

While pervading everything –

Some essence,

Lies in and between

The revelations:

of

Newton, Bohr, Einstein and Bell;

Schrödinger, Dirac and Feynman.

That planets and quarks,

Muons and moons:

Dance to provide us numbers;

To toy with our frail human need –

For binary thought;

For some sense of probability;

For certainty:

Defying any semblance of quaternary thought:

With wave and field,

Particle and negative spin,

Working other dimensions

– all at once!

The source and essence:

Of beauty:

Of feelings, and substances;

Of sensing –

A LIFE

Such perfume as love exudes:

From the complexity of consciousness –

Even collective consciousness –

Grown from proton waves,

Traversing neuronal connections:

Integrated;

Purposeful;

Yet defying sense.

What is locked in these dimensional boxes,

Each without an exit or entrance;

Without spy-holes:

To confirm our theories, beliefs and suspicions?

We are locked in;

Only to internally justified.

Like energy strings;

Conjectured,

Unfit for universal application.

Like atoms concreted into stars;

The constituents of our mind and soul;

While ephemeral –

Deny complete access.

Using sturdier concepts –

Laminar flow, locks and keys;

Bifurcations, turbulence;

Switches and gates:

Opening, closing:

Some influenced by thought,

Some thought producing.

Some changing with observation;

Others by deed,

Some using imagination,

A LIFE

While some pose other views:

Of superposition;

Superstition;

Entanglement,

Magic;

Dimension change;

Sets within and without:

Matrioshki everywhere.

Give us some data,

Consistent with our theory,

And our critical belief can relax.

Then perhaps,

Our sanctimony can ignite.

From boundaries beyond imagination,

To the ultra-microscopic:

Our belief,

Supported by calculation and bias,

Will be comprehended,

But not more than:

The square root of -1.

Thus, 'Zhe' never makes sense,

And needs no meaning:

When believing only boxed-in determinants.

In every dimension,

'Zhe' is in balance.

Despite the rhythm:

The waves of reality,

Are driven large and small;

Whether by attraction,

Repulsion, spin,

Combination, subtraction,

A LIFE

And transformation.

Like thought and spirit:

Essence diffuses,

Throughout all paradigms:

Within and between all dimensions;

Regardless of time.

Since it's obvious that:

$\int ж.n.dt = 0;$

With integral limits of 0 and ∞:

The planets, stars and galaxies;

Bees and humans,

Electrons, and up and down quarks;

Minds and souls,

All MUST accept,

Limited human access.

Conserving indestructible energy pertains;

Regardless of vectors and chaos,

Laminar flow, bifurcation, and turbulence –

With entropy –

Always active;

Always unacceptable,

To the human spirit.

'Zhe' is without intent;

Without portent:

Existing beyond expectation;

Beyond imagination;

Belief unnecessary.

Millions of lifetimes have passed,

Devoted to finding its meaning,

A LIFE

Where none exists.

Reality – an artificial construct –

Is all we have ever had.

Secure in a locked box:

The product of evolving frontiers;

Our hopes and aspirations:

Devoted to deriving meaning,

By egos in search of justification.

So, a question:

Is 'Zhe' interchangeable,

With Spinoza's God?

Understanding neither good nor bad:

Without sainthood or eternal retribution –

Without a voice,

Yet evolving without intention –

Without consensual permission?

A miracle of infinite existence:

Challenged by complicated minds;

Believed unconditionally,

By simple minds,

And blessed,

For being so.

The Quest

Enjoy understanding.

But know that,

The quest for it,

Can excite more.

Essence

Translating

Your nature to mine;

My language to yours:

What essence lost?

Does a '2',

Embody the essence,

Of two frogs,

Or two apples?

What essence is lost,

Translating colour:

Black to white,

And blue to green?

A LIFE

What essence added –

Might transform:

What are two frogs,

Into two apples?

Lying Between the Definable

Only by virtue of,

Its essence

Can 'being' be,

And love exist.

Our Essence

There is an essence

To culture,

And language:

That's part of our being.

Essence and Reality

Only with learning

And experience,

Can we reside

In essence.

The essence:

Basis of all things,

Material, and

Ethereal.

Pervading,

Without number,

Or word:

It's reality eternal.

Pervading all thought,

And all feeling;

With the essence

Of all purpose.

Togetherness

Across this frontier:

No access,

Except the notion

Of another.

Stand together with me:

Sense a silent presence:

Perceived,

Never seen.

PART THREE

CHAPTER THREE

Getting Personal

Shattered Love

I have sought love;
I have sought peace.
I found them both:
Finding some shattered.

The oil of love,
And the water of logic;
Co-exist –
Not to mix.

If yellow can love red;
And green love blue,
Should white and black,
Have their chance?

Restoration

Sleep refreshes -
When running deep
Calm, and peaceful -

It will restore us.

Knowing Nothing?

With ultimate
Understanding,
I can know nothing,
And think no more.

Linger No Longer

By revisiting,
You will not find

What once was:
Alone the present.

Reliability

Prize reliability –
It marks honour:
As wearer
Of a crown.

Entangled `Love

Our love donated –

Left with others:

Flies and soars:

Away – contented.

Separated,

But remaining one –

Entangles,

Like two particles.

Never Relevant?

Imagine your relevance

To others:

Then falsely,

Miss it later.

Cry not,

For that lost respect;

When it never was,

Yours, ever before.

Missed Opportunity?

Parting . . .

Creates missed

Opportunities,

That only hope can project.

Who knows

If fleeting contact

Once was,

A past life – or future to be.

Becoming irrelevant,

After being relevant:

Gift or

Not?

Giving & Taking

Selfless giving:

Is only for

The righteous,

And for the foolhardy.

Demeaning

Generosity,

Follows saying:

'Enough is enough!'

Once the fruit

Has been eaten,

The tree is abandoned

'Til next year.

For humans

With no more

To give:

Abandonment can be forever.

Only the righteous

Recognise their debts,

And will return

With succour.

Breaking Bonds

Even angels,

Can reject and depart,

Yet make those

Who love them cry.

Love's Return?

Once born and sealed,

Love never dies;

It fades unvisited,

But lives on.

Can mutual thought;

Spark its former essence,

Back into life;

Into mind?

Existence

Does the unimaginable

Add,

Or detract,

From our existence?

How to Live Life

Should we all live life,

Supposing to grow?

Or each live life,

Without care?

Defining a Friend

I still miss Tony:

Seventy years on,

From school,

And I need him still!

An indispensable

Compatriot.

A treasure gone:

Still with me.

A Doctor's Demise

My purpose here:

Always to help others:

It sources

My self-esteem.

Must I accept,

As age progresses,

My helping others -

Reverses?

Readiness

Some are born ready;

But most will never be –

Ready,

For a full life.

Imagination

Imaginativeness,

Has its own realm,

While logic

Has another.

Try!

Primitive within,

Our attraction

To beauty and status,

Drives us.

Trying. Hoping,

To gain and achieve,

What is below

Or above us.

Biased by the illusions

Of ourselves:

Our choices,

Can defeat us.

The Blessed

Blessed are the content,

For theirs is the power:

To disturb,

Unfound souls.

Blessed are egoists

Whose drive

And ambition,

Point us far away.

Blessed are the unclean,

For they can teach us

Of love,

And selflessness.

Blessed are the wealthy

Who can teach us

How much more,

The poor possess.

Blessed

Are the bigoted,

As they can turn us

Towards openness.

Blessed are they,

Who give of themselves,

For they deserve

Their righteousness.

Time & Place

When trajectories cross:

The time

May be right,

But the plane different.

Destiny will prescribe

Our trajectory:

The right time,

The right plane.

Which Place?

Crowds,

Have led me into solitude;

And loneliness,

Back into crowds.

Achievement

Aim for self-satisfaction;

Without vanity;

Then –

You can achieve.

Progressing

As moments progress,

They leave stains,

As transient

Blots on memory.

Sexual Gratification

Sex for men –

Self-validating.

Sex for women –

Manipulating.

XX seeks

Future prospect;

XY – sex, love,

And accreditation.

Diverging needs,

Lead to contempt:

Relationships

Then disintegrate.

Multiplying Stress

Youth and poverty:

Multiply stress.

Dispersing,

With age and wealth.

Choose your life:

A life of peace;

A life of discord.

Choice or not a choice?

Leave Hubris Behind?

Lose your

Vanity and ego,

And you achieve,

Ultimate composure.

Then – there will be,

No need for chaos;

No need to try:

Existing as 'me'.

Leave behind your hubris;

Resign it to bad fate;

Live unknown,

And think free.

A LIFE

Be kind:

The sanctimonious

And resentful,

Are living in hell.

Young & Old

For the young:

Dripping with fecundity,

The old watch:

Rye smiles beaming.

Need for desire

Draws an obvious picture;

Made subtle,

By beauty.

Notice me,

Or I die; lonely,

Languishing bereft;

Undesired.

Blame Complexity?

Thoughts and feelings:

All derivatives

Of complexity,

And not real.

Expressed Emotion

Around the mouth,

And eyes,

Micro-moves,

Can radiate significance.

A State of Grace

Coming only as gifts,

The fires

Of passion and faith,

Can consume life.

Once experienced

Through another,

One might find –

Composure.

To be at-one,

With energy fields,

Can defy

Interpretation.

A state of grace,

Is only attained,

Through inherited

Composure.

Within

An angel's shadow:

See beyond,

Ego and acquisition.

Alone?

Born with,

The sensibility we have;

We then die,

Insensible.

As control slips,

And time passes,

It leads to old age

Isolation.

We are born alone,

And die alone;

Then go to whence,

No-one can know.

Breaking Ego

As both ego and privacy

Are broken –

Love awakens,

Resigned.

Simplicity Reigns

Be simple;

Understand simply:

Gain clarity,

Without confusion.

For guiding angels –

All is known;

All is simple:

Clarity shines.

Does Age Defines Us?

Younger women

Seek wealth,

And security;

Or, future potential.

Young men seek:

Love, sex and fidelity;

Older men:

Companionship.

When old,

Look forward to being

Side-lined; left behind;

Infantilised.

Understanding

Understanding,

Comes through custom,

Using experiment,

Or through both.

Shop or Not?

Shopping

Is female territory:

No male in his right mind,

Goes there!

Forsaken Time

As youth abandons age,

And time

Forsakes all:

We advance together.

Suffering?

Many suffer
From stupidity;
Even more
From intelligence.

One Enchanted Evening

Beware of enchantment:
Its biases,
And lies,
Will disenchant you.

Through disenchantment:
See your biases,
And view,
Mistaken belief.

Onward

Discouragement,
Can defeat some,
And s p u r n
The courageous ego on.

A Cause of Discord

Envy,
Diminishes self-worth,
And creates,
Untreatable discord.

Oh Carol(e), I Am But A Fool!

(After Neil Sedaka. 1961)

You might walk by me;
I might walk in;
We might change course –
Or stay the same.

We might say 'Hello',
Or walk by;
Never to know,
What life we have missed.

Strength

For so many,
Their greatest need
Is perhaps,
To possess greater strength.

Those who want it,
Rarely find –
That their greatest strength,
Is to have no need.

PART FOUR

CHAPTER FOUR

Them or Us?

Cultural Mix

Family and neighbours;

Tribes,

Like believers:

Distinguish 'us' from 'them'

Cultures,

Like oil and water,

Form only,

Temporary emulsions.

Enjoy the mix,

Pretending to comply;

To survive

Time together.

No Time?

Impatience,
Reflects time-urgency:
Real haste,
Or failed recognition.

Detachment

The unreliable
Are detached,
By their other priorities.

Chase them
If you will:
Only to procure,
A foregone disappointment.

Nagged

Nagging others
Is not innocent;
It is an
Emotional crime.

Nagging a person –
One who controls,
Can cause more than
Aggravation.

Medical conditions –

Are made worse:
Catastrophic,

Or causing death

A Past Life?

New face,

Or fantasy?

An acquaintance,

From another existence?

Forgiveness

To be forgiven:

Few deserve.

The forgiver,

Gets most benefit.

'The greater good';

And 'public interest':

Are but,

Metaphysical.

Aspects of Sanctimony

Middle-class aspiration,

Can lead to

Content and,

Sanctimony.

Engagement

Most of us

Behave like sheep;

And all in search of

One worthy shepherd.

Most of us,

Need to be like sheep;

Else the rule of law,

Will condemn us.

Engaging?

Can it be true?

The young care not

To engage:

Only to be noticed?

From Prehistory?

With a greater

Need to give than take,

Most humans,

Lack decent design.

Hunter-gatherers,

Designed to take,

Still outnumber,

Those who will give.

Could it be:

Habilis and *Neanderthal*,

Gave . . .

And *sapiens* took?

Why would the astute,

Not see the value,

In their generous

Kindness?

Toddlers' Despair

Drag 'em;

Push 'em;

Console 'em -

Keep all bored kids occupied.

What about learning,

Fascination and

Pleasure,

As young life begins?

Reduce their tantrums,

Their kicking and

Floor contortions,

And bring them peace.

Why Charlie Kirk?

The arrogance

Of youth,

Loaded with emotion;

Less fact and logic.

Their passion,

Not their reason,

Can motivate,

Lethal reactions.

Solitude

Fields of endless

Solitude,

Are awaiting times for

Congregation.

Religion

How to live;

How to love;

And how to die for God:

That is religion.

Insecurity

Avarice and vanity;

Stable insecurity:

Keep life -

Live.

Find & Seek

Every male,

Needs to seek,

A female

With no expectations.

Every female,

Should seek

A man,

With every expectation.

Dreams

The young

Have their dreams and ego;

The old,

Have irrelevance to savour.

Inhumanity

Man's inhumanity to man,

Knows no bounds;

Cares not to have bounds;

And sees them as weaknesses.

Man's inhumanity to man,

In every petty way,

Will demean us,

Making us its retched servants.

Man's inhumanity to man,

Is now cocooned in law and finance:

Said to serve us,

But there to control,

For useful benefit.

Man's inhumanity to man,

Sourced from ego and vanity,

Aims to enslave us,

To its will.

Man's inhumanity to man,

As a vehicle for hate and control,
Rejects love,

And demeans us all.

Man's inhumanity to man:

Knowing that dog will eat dog,

And every man is for himself:

Can rest secure.

A LIFE

In my lifetime,

Man's inhumanity to man,

Brought Bergen-Belsen and Auschwitz,

To every world.

The altruistic and pious,

Knowing of man's inhumanity to man,

But doing nothing –

Can sleep secure in peace.

Even in the shadows of

Man's inhumanity,

I must serve, cure and help,

My fellow man;

Even though he would tread on others,

To reach the exit.

Perhaps there is a reason for

Man's inhumanity to man?

Is it to reveal the unworthy;

To recognise evil:

And thereby recognise,

Loving angels?

Index

0

0 and ∞, 58

A

abandonment, 78

acquaintance, 117

age, 83, 93, 101, 106

aggravation, 116

algorithm, 2

allure, 9

ambition, 86

angels, 38, 79, 103, 134

anger, 21

apples, 62, 63

art, 22, 41

artificial, 60

aspiration, 119

at-oneness, 21

Auschwitz, 133

autistic, 2

avarice, 127

B

beauty, 9, 52, 85, 96

beliefs, 53

Bell, John, Stewart, 51

benevolence, 38

Bergen-Belsen, 133

bias, 18, 56

biases, 108

bigoted, 88

binary, 2, 52

bio-equality, 11

birds, 49

blessed, 8, 60

Bohr, Niels, 51

brick, 32

C

calculation, 56

certainty, 6, 52

chance, 70

chaos, 58, 94

Charlie Kirk, 125

chasm, 29

check-boxes, 2

choice, 22, 93

clarity, 41, 103

cognition, 38

colour, 8, 27, 39, 62

companionship, 104

compatriot, 82

complex, 20

complexity, 32, 53, 97

compliance, 11

composure, 94

composure, 99, 100

conception, 27

confusion, 102

congregation, 126

conjecture, 33

consciousness, 20

constructive, 9

contempt, 92

contortions, 124

control, 24, 101, 131, 132

conversation, 8

cosmos, 51

crown, 72

custom, 105

D

death, 7, 116

deceit, 29

defeat, 85, 109

delusion, 43

demeaning, 77, 132

destiny, 89

destructive, 9

determinants, 56

dignity, 8

dilemma, 13

dimensional, 53

dimensions, 29, 52, 57

Dirac, Paul, 52

discipline, 3, 10

discord, 93, 109

discovery, 15

disenchantment, 108

dormant, 26

dreams, 129

E

education, 10

ego, 9, 94, 102, 109, 129, 131

egoist, 25

Einstein, Albert, 51

emotion, 38, 125

emperors, 36

empires, 11

enchantment, 108

entanglement, 55

entropy, 42

ephemeral, 54

essence, 1, 2, 46, 47, 48, 51, 52, 62, 63, 64, 65, 66, 80

ethereal, 45

expectations, 127

experience, 65

experiment, 105

exploring, 15

F

faith, 99

faithful, 11

false, 34

fame, 8

family, 113

fantasy, 14, 117

fascination, 124

fate, 1, 36, 94

fear, 28

feelings, 53, 97

female territory, 106

feral, 10

Feynman, Richard, 52

fiction, 2

finance, 131

fleeting, 51, 75

focus, 42

foolhardy, 77

forgiven, 117

fragrance, 48

free-thinking, 2

friendship, 5

frogs, 62, 63

frontier, 32, 39, 67

future, 39, 75, 104

G

gaze, 48

generosity, 77

gift, 5

glances, 46

God, 60, 126

grace, 8, 16, 99, 100

guilt, 21

H

haiku, 1, 3

harmony, 16

hate, 29, 132

hell, 24, 95

hierarchical, 2

history, 43

honour, 8, 72

hope, 28, 75

hubris, 39, 94

human existence, 1

humanity, 12

hunter-gathering, 23

I

imagination, 55, 56, 59

imaginativeness, 84

imperfection, 23

indignation, 21

inescapable, 20

infantilised, 104

inhumanity (to man), 38, 130, 131, 132, 133, 134

insecurity, 127

insight, 2, 45

integrated, 53

intelligence, 9, 107

intention, 60

interpretation, 99

J

journey, 6

joy, 28, 39

judgement, 19

justification, 60

K

kings, 36

L

language, 27, 62, 64

law, 120, 131

learning, 65, 124

lies, 108

life, 6, 43, 81, 117

lifetimes, 59

logic, 2, 70, 84, 125

loneliness, 90

love, 1, 48, 53, 64, 69, 70, 73, 79, 87, 92, 126, 132

loyalty, 5

M

magic, 28

mastery, 41

mathematical, 1

matrioshki, 55

maturation, 30

mature minds, 19

meaning, 27, 45

media, 8

memory, 91

men, 92, 104

metaphysical, 118

micro-moves, 98

microscopic, 56

middle-class, 119

minds, 18, 58

miracle, 60

money, 37

moons, 52

muons, 52

music, 46

N

nagging, 116

Neanderthal, 122

negative, 43

newness, 7

Newton, Isaac, 51

night rhythms, 47

noise, 49, 50

notion, 67

O

oil and water, 114

old, 7, 40, 96, 101, 104, 129

openness, 19, 88

opportunities, 75

P

pain, 17

particles, 73

passion, 99, 125

past life, 75

pawns, 36

peace, 69, 93, 124, 133

perfection, 23

permission, 60

poem, 1

politicians, 24

polymath, 2

poor, 87

positive, 43

power, 9, 11, 24, 86

prehistory, 122

pre-occupation, 13

presence, 48, 67

primitive, 23

probability, 52

proton, 53

public interest, 12

Q

questions, 25

R

reactions, 125

realm, 84

religion, 126

resentful, 95

resentment, 21

respect, 10, 74

retribution, 15

revelations, 51

revisiting, 72

rhythm, 57

righteous, 77, 78

righteousness, 88

romantic, 1, 2

S

sainthood, 60

sanctimonious, 95

sapiens, 122

Schrödinger, Erwin, 52

science, 1, 2

scientist, 2

security, 37, 104

self-satisfaction, 90

self-worth, 109

senryu, 3

sensibility, 101

sentient, 1

servants, 130

sex, 92

shadow, 100

shape, 32, 39

shattered, 69

sheep, 119, 120

shepherd, 119

Shock, 28

shopping, 106

shu-ha-ri, 30

silent, 47

smiles, 96

solitude, 15, 90, 126

souls, 16, 58, 86

sparks, 26

species of man, 38

spin, 52, 57

Spinoza, Baruch, 60

spirit, 57, 58

standards, 8

stars, 54, 58

strength, 111

strokes, (cerebral), 42

stupidity, 34, 107

succour, 78

superposition, 55

T

teach, 87

theories, 53

threaten, 43

time, 6, 7, 8, 89, 106, 114, 115

time-urgency, 115

tiredness, 13

trajectory, 89

tranquillity, 13

transported, 6

treasure, 82

tribes, 113

truth, 14

U

understanding, 1, 3, 34, 61

universe, 1

unnoticed, 25

unworthy, 134

V

vain, 25

vanity, 14, 41, 90, 94, 127, 131

vigilance, 42

voices, 50

vulgarity, 10

W

walk by me, 110

wealth, 10, 93, 104

wisdom, 34

Wittgenstein, Ludwig, 33

women, 92, 104

words, 6, 46

Y

youth, 26, 40, 106, 125

Z

Zhe, 51

www.ingramcontent.com/pod-product-compliance
Lightning Source LLC
Chambersburg PA
CBHW052033070526
44584CB00016B/2026